ME ENCANTA LA GIMNASIA/
I LOVE GYMNASTICS

By Ryan Nagelhout   Traducido por Eida de la Vega

Gareth Stevens
PUBLISHING

Please visit our website, www.garethstevens.com. For a free color catalog of all our high-quality books, call toll free 1-800-542-2595 or fax 1-877-542-2596.

Library of Congress Cataloging-in-Publication Data

Nagelhout, Ryan.
I love gymnastics = Me encanta la gimnasia / by Ryan Nagelhout.
  p. cm. — (My favorite sports = Mis deportes favoritos)
Parallel title: Mis deportes favoritos
In English and Spanish.
Includes index.
ISBN 978-1-4824-0852-2 (library binding)
1. Gymnastics — Juvenile literature. I. Nagelhout, Ryan. II. Title.
GV461.3 N34 2015
796.44—d23

First Edition

Published in 2015 by
Gareth Stevens Publishing
111 East 14th Street, Suite 349
New York, NY 10003

Editor: Ryan Nagelhout
Designer: Nick Domiano
Spanish Translation: Eida de la Vega

Photo credits: Cover, p. 1 Katkov/iStock/Thinkstock.com; p. 5 Jupiterimages/BananaStock/Thinkstock.com; p. 7 David Handley/Dorling Kindersley/Getty Images; p. 9, 24 (flip) Tony Wear/Shutterstock.com; p. 13 Amana Images/Thinkstock.com; p. 11 Assembly/Photographer's Choice RF/Getty Images; p. 13 Fuse/Fuse/Getty Images; pp. 15, 24 (mat) Micha Klootwijk/Shutterstock.com; pp. 17, 19 Michael C. Gray/Shutterstock.com; pp. 21, 24 (roll) Alexey Fursov/Shutterstock.com; p. 23 alexkatkov/Shutterstock.com.

Printed in the United States of America

CPSIA compliance information: Batch #CS15GS: For further information contact Gareth Stevens, New York, New York at 1-800-542-2595.

Contenido

Volteretas y saltos mortales. 4

La seguridad es muy importante 12

¡Relájate!. 16

Nuevos movimientos. 20

Palabras que debes saber 24

Índice 24

Contents

Roll and Flip 4

Safety First. 12

Loosen Up! 16

New Moves 20

Words to Know 24

Index. 24

¡Es hora de
hacer gimnasia!

It is time for gymnastics!

Aprendo a dar vueltas.
Se llaman volteretas.

I learn how to roll.
This is called tumbling.

7

Aprendo a dar
saltos mortales.

I learn how to do flips.

No me pongo
calcetines.

I do not wear
any socks.

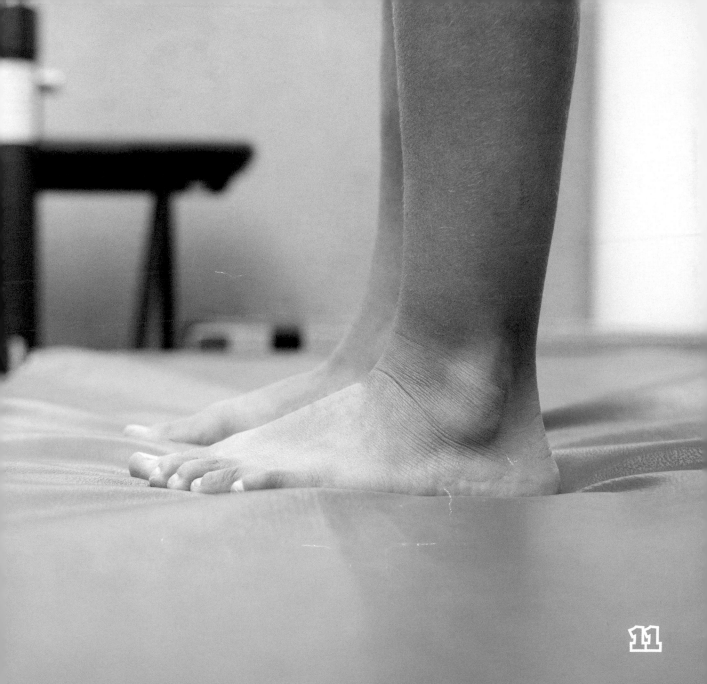

Pongo colchonetas
en el suelo.

I put down mats.

13

Las colchonetas
me protegen.

The mats keep me safe.

Tienes que relajar
el cuerpo.

You need to keep
your body loose.

17

¡Tienes que ser fuerte!

You have to be strong!

19

Me encanta aprender
cosas nuevas.

I love to learn
new things.

21

¡Ven a entrenar
con nosotros!

Come train with us!

23

Palabras que debes saber/ Words to Know

el salto mortal/
flip

la colchoneta/
mat

la voltereta/
roll

Índice / Index

colchonetas/mats 12, 14

proteger/keep safe 14

saltos mortales/flips 8

volteretas/tumbling 6